Table of Contents

Introduction

Wednesday 3 September 2015. Broomfield Hospital, Chelmsford

It will probably be nothing. That's what we've been telling ourselves for the past week, although I'd be lying if I said that the appointment hadn't been constantly on my mind. Jo is mildly concerned about the lump she found a couple of weeks ago. But, as our youngest daughter is four months old and our eldest daughter is still only three, Jo puts the abnormality down to the "wear and tear", as she calls it, of having been pregnant three times in under four years. She found the lump under her right breast when she was in the shower. Her body was starting to return to its pre-pregnancy shape and, being fairly diligent at checking herself, she's fairly sure it's a recent development. She did the right thing and contacted the local GP straight away. During the examination, he expressed mild concern but said it could be a number of things and he referred her to the breast specialist at our local hospital. That's where we are now. Jo is reading "Town and Country" magazine and I'm distractedly skimming through "Esquire", my mind trying not to second guess what might be about to happen. I make a quip about her choice of reading material, and she shoots me a side glance with the right side of her top lip slightly raised, her eyes partially narrowed – a look she's perfected on me over the years.

Twenty minutes later, we are called into the breast surgeon's office. He quizzes Jo about when she discovered the lump and any side effects she may be experiencing. We have a four-month-old baby, a toddler and a three-year-old, so it's hard for Jo to identify any physical symptoms, other than general fatigue. The surgeon examines Jo and expresses concern as to the shape, size and feel of the lump. We are shown into a separate room where Jo is told to get into a surgical gown. And then we wait for her to have a scan and a biopsy on the lump.

*

Two hours later

We weren't prepared for this. It's less than two hours after we were called into the initial appointment and now Jo is lying on a hospital bed, desperate for the painkillers to kick in after having had two painful biopsies, one on her breast and one on her lymph nodes. I'm clutching her hand but she's squirming with discomfort and trying in vain to find a comfortable position on the bed. The intensity of her tears has eased but they are still welling in her eyes, and the suddenness of the biopsy procedure and the pain it has caused her has caught me off-guard and I'm struggling to know what to say. I attempt some reassuring words, 'It's going to be okay. Whatever happens, you'll get through it.' But the speed and unexpected nature of what is happening is overwhelming and I'm not sure whether her tears are as a result of the pain, the realisation that

Originally from the north of England, David Peart now lives in a village in Essex with his three daughters. He is a widowed husband to Joanne, who died in July 2019.

He has previously written two children's books to help his daughters during their grieving process. *I Want to Hug Mummy*, and *It's Okay to Feel Happy* are now being used to help other children and families who have experienced loss. That inspired him to write a book from his point of view that can help other people who have related experiences—not just bereavement but other disruptive events.

This book is dedicated to everyone who has helped me put the pieces of my life back together. To everyone who has supported me, advised me, and listened to me; thank you.

David Peart

RESILIENCE

A Dad's Journey Through Grief

AUSTIN MACAULEY PUBLISHERS[TM]

LONDON • CAMBRIDGE • NEW YORK • SHARJAH

A CIP catalogue record for this title is available from the British Library.

ISBN 9781035831753 (Paperback)
ISBN 9781035831760 (ePub e-book)
ISBN 9781035831777 (Audiobook)

www.austinmacauley.com

First Published 2024
Austin Macauley Publishers Ltd®
1 Canada Square
Canary Wharf
London
E14 5AA

I would like to thank the editorial board at Austin Macauley for offering me the opportunity of publication and to everyone at the organisation for making it a reality.

there is something very wrong, the shock of what's happened to her in the last two hours, or a combination of all three.

*

Fifty minutes later

We were assured the results would be back within the hour and we've only had to wait fifty minutes before we are called back into the breast surgeon's office. The initial pain has subsided in Jo's breast and under her armpit, but she says that a deep soreness has already set in, and I have to carefully manoeuvre her off the bed and onto her wobbly legs. 'I just want to get this gown off,' she mutters as we slowly walk into the office. The sternly professional look on the surgeon's face stops us both mid-step.

'Oh no,' Jo mutters. 'I don't believe it.'

'Please, take a seat.' He gestures to the chairs on the opposite side of his desk.

He is calm in his delivery of the news, but firm and clear. From the scans and the biopsy, he gives Jo an initial diagnosis of stage three breast cancer. The lymph nodes appear clear so that is a positive. And that is about all we are told; he tells us that imparting too much additional information at this stage is futile as we are unlikely to process or remember it. We are to go home, digest the information as best we can, stay off the internet to make sure we don't do any self-prognosis, and come back to the hospital in two days where he can talk us through the next steps.

Our lives have changed, immediately and completely, and nothing could have prepared us for that.

Friday 4 September 2015

We are back at the hospital, sipping on coffee in the waiting room. We're not browsing through magazines this time; my hand is gently resting on top of Jo's as we both sit in silence, waiting to be called in to see the surgeon. I'm desperate for this appointment to be over so we can be given a plan. The most difficult aspect of the last two days has been the unknown of what's ahead. That has been challenging and has overwhelmed thoughts about anything else. Nothing can prepare you for a single moment that de-rails the routine of a life which was framed with the order, structure and routine of family and work life and then suddenly you have no idea of the path ahead. Jo has understandably been quiet and reflective at home. Her thoughts have naturally been consumed with the diagnosis and I've been doing my best to put on a calm and cheerful demeanour for the sake of our daughters. At one point, as we were quietly having dinner after the girls had gone to bed, Jo muttered an apology that she'd not organised anything for my fortieth birthday, which was the following week. 'Don't worry about it,' I replied and took her hand as tears welled up in her eyes. 'It's really not important and there will be plenty of other birthdays to celebrate.'

*

The surgeon begins by confirming the diagnosis of stage three breast cancer and he then talks us through the likely course of treatment. Surgery to remove the breast, chemotherapy and possibly a round of radiotherapy depending upon how well the treatment goes. 'I will be in control of your life for about a year,' he says frankly to Jo. 'It will be a hard year and you

14

will need plenty of support, but then you will have your life back,' he ends reassuringly, handing Jo a brochure about reconstructive surgery. 'No pressure and no rush but I want to do the operation as soon as possible, so take a look at some of the options that will be available to you. Reconstructive procedures are not without risk, especially because the body will be recovering and healing from the operation. If you want to proceed with reconstruction, we will have to assess the risks at the time and take into account how well your body is healing post the surgery. However, there are a number of options available, and it may be something you'd like to think about.'

And then came the moment that is central to everything that subsequently happened in our lives. The surgeon gestured towards a room adjoining his office. 'As I will be doing the surgery on you, I'd like to know exactly who I am operating on. There may be old operations or injuries that you have forgotten about or are unaware of. There is a full body MRI scan machine in the room next door. The nurse will set it up for you. Get that done, both of you go and get a coffee and then we'll get the mastectomy booked in and confirm next steps.'

*

An hour later

When we are called back into the surgeon's office, we are both instantly aware that the atmosphere has changed. His relaxed demeanour has become more serious, and his tone has altered and become more tense. We don't say a word and sit

15

down in silence, our gazes fixed on his stern face as he holds the images of the scan in front of him.

'I'm afraid I can't operate on you. The cancer has spread; it's already in your spine.'

*

Four years later
Saturday 15 June 2019

I open the blinds and the glowing warmth of early summer streams into the bedroom. I barely notice. I sit back on the bed, Jo propped up beside me, breathing quickly and shallowly, her hands resting on an uncomfortably bloated stomach. She's only been back at home for a week after spending four days in hospital having her stomach drained. It had bloated to a size greater than when she was fully pregnant due to fluid building up and putting immense pressure on her organs. That hospital visit nearly broke her; the pain and lingering discomfort of having her stomach drained whilst lying on her side in a hospital bed for four days broke her spirit. When I was finally able to discharge her, I had carefully eased her out of the bed and supported her as we slowly walked out of the ward. At one point on the way to the car, she stopped, stared pleadingly at me and made me promise that no matter how bad things got, I would never let her go back into hospital and have that procedure done to her again. Thankfully, her spirits lifted as soon as she got home, but she has been bed-ridden ever since. Her liver has fully failed, and the fluid built back up in her stomach within days of her returning home.

I feel physically sick. An anxious, stomach-churning sensation that is making the pressure in my temples pulse. We are trying to ready ourselves for what we are about to do. But, in truth, nothing can prepare us. We've decided it's the only option; the best way to protect our daughters.

I get out of bed again and open the windows. We are fortunate to have the tranquillity of a field bordering the house and Jo has taken comfort from the sound of the wind rustling through the wheat crop. It's helped to calm her during a period of intense pain and discomfort, and I already know it is a sensory memory that will remain with me forever.

Our daughters come into the bedroom at intervals. They are seven, five and four years old. For almost four years, we have lived in three-month cycles of appointments, treatment and the agonising wait for results. The treatments are now at an end; Jo has exhausted all options and she has weeks of her life remaining. The failed liver and yellow tinge in her eyes mean that what we are about to do as parents cannot wait.

During Jo's illness, we have been as open with our children as possible, whilst being protective. They knew when their mum was having treatment and they knew that would mean she would spend some time in bed recovering. They deserve to remain children for as long as possible and we desperately wanted the innocence of their childhood to remain for as long as possible. But, since the day of the diagnosis, we have always known what the end point would be, we just didn't know when it would come. Our lives changed on the words, 'Your cancer is incurable. The goal is to manage it as best we can in order to prolong your life for as long as possible.' Now the time has come, and it will be my job going forward to maintain as much of our daughters' individual and collective enjoyment of childhood as possible. But they will be growing up with the magical innocence of childhood having gone.

The girls sit, side-by-side at the foot of the bed. Even though they are well used to Jo being in bed for short periods of time, they instinctively know that something has changed.

'We have something we need to talk to you about.'

When Jo's voice waivers and she can't say anymore, I take over. We tell our daughters that the treatment their mummy has been having has now stopped working and there are no alternatives left. We tell them that means Mummy will die soon and that there is nothing we can do now to stop that from happening. It is no one's fault but we have to prepare for her not being with us. We deliberately don't use the words "go to sleep" or "pass away" as there can be no ambiguity in what we are telling them. 'Mummy is going to die, but she will always love us and will always be in our memory and we will all do our best to make her proud.'

*

Saturday 6 July 2019. Farleigh Hospice, Chelmsford.

Jo has been in the hospice for ten days and the last place I expected to be is in a local bakery collecting an assortment of sandwiches, cakes and biscuits. A collection such as this would normally send the senses into a merry dance of anticipation. Not today though; I don't have much of an appetite. However, it's Jo's final wish, something she insisted I try and make happen since the day she moved into the hospice. A tea party in her room; her daughters and me around a table, eating sandwiches and cakes with her – if she can manage to get out of the bed to which she has been almost totally contained.

During her time in the hospice, Jo has only been able to get out of bed with the aid of a walking stick. She has occasionally managed to get to the bathroom by herself but tends to need the assistance of a nurse or me to do so. But today, she somehow gets out of bed, gently dismisses my offer of help and walks unaided to the table in the centre of the room. The boxes of food are opened and the girls tuck in. Jo even manages to eat part of a sandwich and some cake after only being able to consume ice lollies for the past week. The episode is a graphic example of the power of will. This is what she desired as her final life experience, a final memory of the whole family together. And, despite her crushing frailty, she manages to do it. For a full twenty minutes, she sits and talks to me and the girls. Not full sentences but breathless words that are slowly, and with great effort, formed into sentences. And then, when even her will can't keep her sitting unaided in the chair any longer, she stands up and shuffles back to the bed. The girls and I watch her as she falls to sleep almost instantly. But she did it; she created a memory that will be hugely significant to our children throughout their lives, and it is a day that they already frequently talk to me about. As they get older, the significance of that day and that event will only increase.

For the next hour, the girls take it in turns to lie on the bed next to their mum, playing with the remote control which raises and lowers the bed at varying speeds. Jo keeps her eyes closed but I'm sure there is a faint smile on her lips.

When it is time for us to leave, I lean down to kiss her forehead. She partially opens her eyes and looks at me.

'That's it, David,' she whispers. 'That's what I wanted and now I can go in peace. From now on, it's only you who comes to see me.'

*

Thursday, 11 July 2019. Farleigh Hospice

After spending the day at Jo's bedside, I'm called back to the hospice shortly after returning home. I'm told to hurry as Jo's breathing patterns have changed. But it's rush hour and it takes me half an hour longer than usual to make the journey. I try to keep the "what ifs" out of my head. If this is the end, my wife is not going to die without me by her side.

I do arrive at the hospice in time, but the nurses are clear. Jo's breathing pattern indicates that end of life is imminent. I'm told that, before death, the last sense to fail is hearing and so, for an hour and a half I hold Jo's hand and talk about as many memories as I can. How we met, our first date, the first flat we bought together, holidays, our wedding, the birth of our children, how she'd perfected "that look".

And then, at 6.40pm, Jo exhales for the final time and I sit, not wanting to let go of her hand as my tears flow. I'm not a gifted enough writer to begin to express in words the power and mixture of emotions that flood through me.

Part One

The introduction to this book is a raw, open and honest account of the events surrounding my wife's death that will remain part of my psyche forever. I'm not a clinical professional; not a doctor, psychologist or counsellor. What I am is a bereaved father of three young daughters, with a full-time job, a household to run and sanity to maintain. Jo died on 11 July 2019 and the loss we suffered as a family came only a few months before a global COVID pandemic sent us all into an extended lockdown and transformed the world and how we had to live our lives. Just at the time when every piece of professional advice was to provide my daughters with as much stability and normality as possible, all that disappeared and left me grieving my wife and worrying about the futures of my daughters.

The importance of mental health and the breaking down of the taboos surrounding it have received significantly more publicity and have become higher profile in recent years. In particular, men's mental health and wellbeing has received some high-profile focus because of the willingness of celebrities who have experienced loss, grief and mental health issues to raise awareness and highlight the importance of men talking about their problems, seeking help and expressing the grief they are dealing with. There has also been a significant increase in the science behind the emotions we feel as humans. The science behind how the brain works, the chemicals the body produces that control the way we feel, how the imbalance of negative emotions, depression, anxiety and so on are biologically formed and scientifically work. That is all hugely important, and fascinating, and understanding these things from a medical and scientific way goes a long way to help people understand the emotions they are feeling.

However, this book is not about that. I have no background, expertise or qualifications to talk with any authority on such things. My intention is to purely reflect on and highlight the thoughts, feelings and emotions I experienced. In doing so, I hope the authentic account will resonate with people experiencing similar emotions, whatever the individual reason or trigger behind them. This book is about my experience and is absolutely not meant to be a blueprint for the emotions that others may experience. My hope is to raise awareness of the devastating impact that a range of negative emotions can cause – emotions that a huge number of us deal with at some point in our lives. I'm writing from the understanding and experience of a man—a father and widower—however, I hope the thoughts within the book can help in some way with anyone who is experiencing negative emotions. I'm conscious that men typically don't have much of a voice or confidence when it comes to expressing their emotions. They can certainly feel compelled to suppress what they are feeling, whether to save face at work and pretend that nothing is wrong, or to be the "strong" one at home with their family. I believe that men should feel accepted, and feel it is acceptable, to talk about how they are feeling, not only without judgement but also with an understanding of why they are experiencing the emotions they are struggling with and how to deal with them. All I can say from my experience is that this needs to be normalised, because it is just that. It is completely normal to experience negative emotions, as natural as it is to experience positive ones because all those variants are simply emotions which come and go. Of course, experiencing negative emotions is at best, not pleasant, and at times it may be almost downright impossible to get out of bed and face the world. But we are all resilient by nature and we can learn to acknowledge and experience the negative emotions as waves that approach and then wash over us – rather than drown us. It is also remarkable just what we can do when we are at our lowest point. It is preferable to find ways as early as possible to equip yourself to deal with the emotions that are affecting you, to allow an understanding and provide the mechanisms to cope with what you are experiencing. However, inner resilience is a powerful trait and one that can be transformational when it kicks in. I apologise for the repetitive comment, but it is important to repeat that none of this content is clinical advice or backed up by qualified psychological study. It is all personal observation and thoughts from someone who has lived through it. It's about what happened to me in my life, the challenges I faced and the resilience that built up in me.

I'm a relatively private person, however the personal impact my experience had on me made me want to share it and hopefully make people more aware of three pivotal things that took me about seven years to realise. Firstly, that in the face of extreme adversity, just how emotionally resilient a person can be. Secondly, that it's okay and absolutely normal not to feel happy. And thirdly; even if you've lost someone you love or you are experiencing a range of negative emotions, it is also okay to be happy. If I have one wish for the book, it would be for it to help someone who has, or is, suffering emotionally, whether due to grief or some other traumatic event, because we all have periods in our lives when adversity strikes and we suffer. If the book can help just one other person, then it will have been well-worth writing.

*

Telling my daughters that their mum was going to die was the hardest thing I've ever done. But, individually and jointly as a couple, Jo and I always took the approach through her illness of being open and honest with our daughters, whilst being as protective as we could. It was a difficult balance to strike but one that we felt was important. We tried to provide enough honest information to inform what the illness was and the impact of the treatment, without imparting too much knowledge that would scare them into wondering if their mum would still be there after they returned from a day at school. So, even at their young ages, they knew when their mum was having treatment and they knew that if she couldn't join us on an outing—which was rarely the case—it was because she was feeling too poorly or she needed time to recover from a treatment. It provided a base knowledge of what was going on, albeit without any real understanding or comprehension as to the severity and future implications for the family. We openly used the word "cancer" as we did not want there to be any opportunity later in their lives for our daughters to ask me, 'Why didn't you tell us what was going on?' We maintained their enjoyment of childhood as much as possible and did as many activities as a family unit that we could. Since

Jo died, I have also done my best at carrying that on. Some days I admit to not doing much, other than letting them play together at home or having quiet screen time. But, even then, it's always on my mind that I just want them to be enjoying childhood.

Taking that relatively open approach throughout Jo's illness also meant that we didn't hesitate from telling our daughters that she was going to die. There could be no ambiguity for them, no "falling to sleep", or "passing away". They needed to know that the day their mum moved into the hospice was the last time she would be in the family home. I'd like to think that how we dealt with things and explained the situation helped us to have positive experiences as a family during the times we visited the hospice; especially when we fulfilled Jo's wish of having a tea party. The girls wanted to visit and wanted to be with their mum – they were apprehensive about going to the hospice, but not scared, and that was important for us creating those memories. I've no evidence for knowing any of this for certain, but I'd like to think that the approach we took with our daughters allowed them to build up just enough inner resilience to allow them to deal with those final few weeks and make those final experiences together happen.

It was an action of our middle daughter during the week following us telling her and her sisters that Jo was going to die, that made us proud and deeply upset at the same time. She was five years old at the time and her class had been preparing for "show and tell" in the afternoon. Our daughter had spent the morning painting a picture that she was going to present to the class and talk about. When it came for her turn, she stood up from her desk and walked to the front of the class holding her picture. However, on the way, she paused, put the painting down, stood facing the class and said, 'During my show and tell, I want to let you all know that my mummy is going to die soon. Have you got any questions?'

After the teacher had regained some composure, she encouraged my daughters' classmates to ask any questions they had, and she helped her to answer them as best she could. 'When?' 'Why?' 'How do you know?' And, when there were no more questions, my daughter went back to her desk and got on with the rest of her day.

It was a huge shock for me and Jo when the headmistress called us to explain what had happened and, of course, we were desperate to see our daughter and make sure she was okay. We worried that we'd shared too much information but the teacher told us that it had been empowering for her to do what she did and reassured us that if she hadn't wanted to do it, she wouldn't have. What it told both of us, was that she had exhibited a resilient trait that we hoped would allow her to keep being open and confident to talk about things after Jo died. And, so far, our daughters have done that. They have their own personalities and their own levels of self-reflection, but they all openly talk about their mum and that is hugely important for their grieving process and their mental well-being.

Part Two

Your Lost Self –
It's Okay Not to Be Happy

Anyone who has experienced negative emotions can tell you just how psychologically damaging and physically draining they can be. For anyone living with those emotions on a daily basis, those symptoms manifest themselves to an entirely new level.

Although I didn't realise it at the time, the day Jo was diagnosed with incurable cancer was the day I started grieving. Even though I wasn't ready to accept what was ultimately going to happen, my sub-conscious mind knew what the end point was going to be. I just didn't know when that time would arrive. For the next four years, until her death, we lived a constant cycle of treatment, scans and results and I lived in a semi-permanent state of flight or fight. I was working full time, I was a father, husband and carer and had to do most of the housework. No matter where I was physically, no matter what situation I was in socially or professionally, my sub-conscious self was elsewhere, consumed with a variety of emotions and the situation of what life had thrown at us. During those four years, I felt like a very different person than before Jo's diagnosis. That moment of diagnosis changed everything for us as individuals and as a couple. From our goals and aspirations as a married couple with a young family, to the physical and emotional dynamic of our relationship as husband and wife. Let me be clear, the love I felt never faded, but it did alter. The person I met and who I got to love, live with and create a family with, was the most fun-loving, free spirited person I'd ever met. After her diagnosis, I got to love her for so much more as well – the person she became after she got ill. Nonetheless, a seismic personal change had occurred and the speed it happened caused me significant mental trauma.

Over the months that followed Jo's diagnosis, our family situation became my sole purpose and it permanently felt overwhelming. Whether I was at work, at home, on the commute to work, out with friends or trying to exercise, my mind was full of worry and turmoil. It never had a chance to settle and rest. How were we going to manage ourselves and our daughters through it? How were our daughters going to cope, not only after their mum had gone but during all stages of her illness? Would they be okay at school and would their academic learning and emotional development be affected during the incredibly important formative years? Would they retreat into themselves and shy away from social interaction? Was Jo going to live her remaining life in pain? Would we have to modify the house to accommodate her needs if she became confined to bed or need use of a wheelchair? The cancer having spread through the spine could have led to any number of physical impairments. Would any of the treatments work? How long did I have left with my wife? Could I handle myself and my emotions well enough to keep going? Would I remain physically and psychologically strong enough to look after Jo and the girls? Could I keep a clear enough head at work and learn to compartmentalise my life enough to allow me to focus on my job and function at an acceptable level to me and my employer? How was I going to care for my wife, children and the unknown that faced us every day? Those are some of the thoughts that were constantly at the forefront of my mind, no matter whether I was going to bed, waking up or going about my day, they consumed my mind. There were the traumatic experiences of treatment days; seeing Jo suffer, then recover in bed. And then the anxious wait for scan results every three months which would show if the body had responded well to the treatment or if there had been an escalation of cancer cells.

When I reflect on my experience, self-realisation about the extent to which I was being affected by all these things occurred about four months before Jo died, when I was sitting in my car in the car park of my local swimming pool. I had driven there after work for a gentle swim because every day for three years people told me I had to look after myself and carve out some "me" time. It was dark, raining and cold and I sat in the car for two hours, mentally and physically exhausted. One of the aspects of Jo's illness that we found the most challenging was not being able to control what came after her diagnosis. Doctors, chemo nurses, treatments, scan and result regimes dictated how we lived and what we could and couldn't do. I realise now that I focused too much attention and wasted far too much emotional energy thinking and worrying about things outside my control. But, as these things directly affect someone you love and have an impact on your family unit, not dwelling on the unknown or uncontrollable is incredibly difficult and something I never managed to do. I attempted to focus on the aspects of our lives that we still could control; however, as a conscious, decision-making human, I found it very difficult to have so much of our lives that we weren't in control of. But, over time, I came to realise that no matter how much we would like to control the "outside" world and everything that happens to us during our everyday lives, it is something we simply can't do. What we can do is try and control how we internally handle those situations; how we choose to react and respond to the adversities of life, or even the relatively mundane aspects of life if they are also causing stress or anxiety. I frequently reminded myself that although I couldn't control the uncontrollable, I could control how I chose to conduct myself. The traumatic event that had affected our family was certainly influencing my life, but I did not want it to define my life and the way I tried to ensure that was by trying to focus as much of my attention and energy on the aspects of mine, Jo's and our children's lives that I could control.

Consciously focusing my energy in that way allowed me to manage and organise mine and my family's lives, work full-time and be a husband and carer. However, as time went on and the stress of the situation gradually increased, I realised that my mind was not in control. I was operating on autopilot, and it was mentally and physically exhausting me. Even though I channelled my physical energy into things I could control, my mind was still consumed with thoughts and worries about what might lie ahead for us. I desperately hope I did a decent job as a parent during that time, but I realise that for a considerable amount of time, even though I was always doing my best, I was not fully present as my mind was always elsewhere. In many ways, I had become an actor. I didn't have my head in the sand, and I wasn't in denial at what was happening to Jo; however, I felt as if I had to permanently act positively in front of her and our daughters. I felt I needed to at least appear to be positive and upbeat as much as possible to enable them to keep positive. I did allow myself certain periods of "letting go", but those were rare and, as time went on, the pressure of the situation became increasingly draining. For the majority of the time, for almost four years, I was acting very much unlike how I was feeling.

Back to the swimming pool car park and, instead of going for a swim, I looked up local counsellors and made contact with one who specialised in grief counselling. For me, that moment of self-awareness, the acknowledgement and acceptance that I was struggling, was the pivotal point at which the process of rebuilding could begin.

Counselling has been a hugely important factor in my life over the past two years. I started my sessions in the months leading up to my wife's death and they helped me immeasurably in dealing with the huge range of emotions I was experiencing of being a father, husband, carer and full-time worker. Since my wife's death, the sessions have helped me put the pieces of my life back together.

That is a testimonial I wrote about a year after Jo's death and the words have even more meaning for me now than I realised at the time. The counselling sessions helped me recognise, understand and acknowledge the emotions I was experiencing which helped equip me mentally with the psychological tools that would help me handle the challenges I faced. That said, there is no magic wand, no single word or sentence makes everything better and a counsellor can't magically make everything okay. It takes an open mind and a desire to listen and, above all, the will to work at helping yourself. If you have a constructive counselling session and then go home and approach things in exactly the same way you have been, then you're unlikely to get much benefit. I know from personal experience that it is sometimes an entire psychological journey in itself to reach a point where you feel positive enough to back yourself in trying new things and attempt to view emotions in a different way – certainly how you let emotions affect you. That all takes time and practice.

*

Recognising and Acknowledging Emotions

When you lose a loved one, lose your job, experience a relationship break up or go through any period in your life that is dominated by negative emotions, it is easy to feel like a victim. 'Why has this happened to me? What have I done to deserve this?' After a profoundly impactful moment soon after Jo died when this happened to me, I tried very hard not to feel like that or view life in that way. Feeling angry and bitter at life itself or towards other people made me feel significantly worse in that moment of experiencing the emotion and for a considerable time afterwards. I fully appreciate that it is very difficult not to view life as being unfair when you lose someone you love, or when you are consumed by emotions that you feel you don't deserve to be experiencing. The mind frequently wanders to that state where you can wallow in feeling low and depressed as to what life has taken from you. It is a mixture of bitterness and resentment at life and the frame of mind where you can justify feeling like a victim. Thankfully, I didn't experience this emotion on many occasions, but when I did, I found it particularly damaging as it stopped me feeling positive about the things in my life I should have been grateful for. My children, my parents, my friends, my job and my health.

My most profound experience of the "why me"? was actually quite fleeting, but very intense and shocked me acutely. About two weeks after Jo died, I was in the car, driving home after dropping the girls off at school. A radio show was running a daily competition where people would phone in and nominate a person they believed deserved to win a luxury holiday. The radio hosts called a lady who had recently lost her husband and had been left a widow of two teenage children. I welled up whilst listening to her harrowing story and, after she'd finished speaking, one of the radio hosts broke down in tears and said it was one of the saddest things she'd ever heard. My reaction to that was involuntary, instantaneous, highly emotional and totally caught me off guard. I shouted, 'Hold on, if you think that's sad, listen to this. My wife was ill for four years with incurable cancer and I'm now a single dad of three girls who are seven, five and four. They have lost their mum.'

How shocking! How selfish! That outburst shocked me profoundly, so much so that seconds later I was crying and apologising to the woman and the radio host. It was certainly among the most intense emotions I've experienced through my grief cycle. It made me feel physically sick; not for long, but the effect on my physical state was significant. I felt guilty for weeks after it, frequently apologising to the lady in my head. In some way though, I think that outburst—whilst I wouldn't recommend it—was also purging in a way. I've frequently thought about the unfairness that so many life events throw at people. However, that personal episode was the only time the "why me"? state has affected me so deeply. Perhaps the intensity of it shocked my body and mind so profoundly that it doesn't want to experience it again. Perhaps it was because I could relate to the lady's story so acutely it made me think, *Gosh, that's the situation I'm now in,* and I involuntarily reacted to that. I'm hypothesising as I've no way of knowing the actual reason for my reaction; however, throughout everything I've experienced over the past seven years, it was certainly among the most intense emotions.

*

My memory of that moment, and of a significant amount of my life and experiences at that time, is of a person that doesn't seem like me at all. So much so, that my memories of that time; collecting Jo's belongings from the hospice, contacting the funeral director, planning her funeral and writing and reading her eulogy at the service – all those things almost feel like it was someone else who did them. Those memories highlight to me how trauma, loss, grief, shock and living in a mental state consumed by negative emotions, can make you into a person you don't recognise. It took me a long time to realise I was living in a kind of bubble; a necessary one at the time as it was a mechanism that allowed me to carry on being a father, husband and worker in the face of significant adversity. However, it was damaging to the psyche and I was fortunate to have the self-realisation as to what was going on and to seek professional help to start to address the issues. I also think it was hugely important for me to have contacted a counsellor before Jo died. I wanted to set the support up beforehand as I didn't know what mental state I would be in afterwards. If I hadn't made contact with my counsellor and hadn't put in place a regular series of counselling sessions, would I have done it after Jo died? I was so consumed with events that happened afterwards; the funeral, the wake, registering the death, contacting service providers to change the names on bills. All my emotional focus was on my daughters in the immediate aftermath of losing their mum and I'm honestly not sure if I'd ever have found space to put myself or my needs first or had the time or emotional energy to find and contact a counsellor. And that thought scares me.

*

Three years have passed since Jo died (at the time of writing this book) and now, when I feel the "why me"? victim state begin to manifest, I deal with it in a different way than the period that initially followed Jo's death. At that point, I spent a lot of time looking at photos of my daughters that were saved on my phone. It was a way to focus, however briefly, on something that made me happy. It was a rudimentary way of my brain trying to find something to focus on that was counter to the overwhelming feelings of negativity that were overwhelming me. For instance, going back to work after my period of bereavement leave was a struggle, and quite honestly something I wasn't mentally ready for. The thought of the train commute to London was something that made me feel uneasy because of the physical distance it was putting between me and my daughters, and I spent most of the time on the train trying to distract myself either by listening to an audiobook or scrolling through photos on my phone. The fleeting distraction those actions provided soon evaporated when I got off the train and it took a long time to rebuild myself to the point where I was comfortable doing the commute again.

When the "why me"? now starts to figure in my thoughts, I also try and practice gratitude. When you experience something like loss, it is very easy to lose sight of and forget the things you have in your life to be grateful for. It is by no means a daily habit I have formed but I do focus more frequently on the things in my life I am grateful for and I find that this especially helps when key life events occur. My daughters are still young and they have their whole lives ahead of them. That is an exciting thought for me, however it also means that the majority of key life events are still to come and doing those without their mum to witness them and help them through the tough ones, can be difficult to think about. There is always a wish that, 'Jo should be here to see this.' My eldest daughter going to secondary school open days or scoring her first goal for her football team. The first time my younger two daughters performed on stage in a theatre production. Carol concerts, nativity plays, weddings of relatives, family holidays; the list goes on and will increasingly get bigger as my daughters get older and these key life events increase. It is at these times when it particularly helps me to practice gratitude. Yes, I wish that Jo was here to witness these things and be here for our daughters, but reminding myself of the things I am grateful for in my life, and consciously trying to feel the gratitude for those things, helps to stop me overthinking and brings me back to the present moment.

*

Physical Effects of Emotional Stress

I'm not qualified or have the experience to analyse the techniques and nuances of how counselling works. What I can say, is that for me, counselling helped me to understand the range of emotions I was experiencing in the months preceding and following my wife's death. Acknowledging that every day I was going to feel some element of grief—or indeed, numerous elements of grief—made me more self-aware, more understanding and more able to deal with the emotions when they arose. What took me longer to recognise and fully appreciate was how my emotional state was affecting me physically.

From a young age, I swam at a relatively high level and as a teenager I competed at national level in swimming and at junior international level in biathlon and triathlon events. During university, I ran my first marathon and so sport, health and overall fitness has always been an important aspect of my life. In the months preceding Jo's diagnosis, I was training for a marathon, so it shocked me when, only a matter of weeks after Jo's diagnosis, I found myself unable to run two or three miles before becoming exhausted. And I lost all motivation to make the effort to even go to a swimming pool, let alone swim. The more I tried to run, the more difficult it became and the harder I was on myself for not being able to exercise properly. I was being told constantly that I had to keep fit and exercise because of the physical and psychological benefits it provides. But I simply couldn't run for very long before having to stop, and those physical symptoms got increasingly worse over the months and years that followed. Living in a semi-permanent state of flight or fight for that length of time not only took a toll mentally but also manifested with acute physical symptoms. I was on my feet all day; getting my daughters ready for school, commuting to work, doing my job, looking after my children, caring for my wife, cleaning the house, cooking, doing three bedtimes. And all this was done with a mind full of worry and uncertainty. No wonder that when I tried to go for a run, my body wouldn't let me. It needed to rest, and it was if it was saying to me, 'Are you kidding? There is a half hour window where you are on your own and free to do what you want and you want to go for a run? Sit down and rest.' But if I did try and rest, I invariably felt guilty for not making better use of the time.

I also struggled to read. I have always been an avid reader and did an English Literature degree because reading and the study of books has always given me so much pleasure. However, I found that I could barely read a sentence, let alone a page without my mind wandering. I would re-read the same words a number of times before giving up, and if I tried to remember what I'd read, I struggled to recall the details. This symptom lasted a long time and some of the personal development markers I set for myself a year or so after Jo died, were the moments when I was able to read a page of a book again, then read more consistently and then be able to recall the details of what I'd read. In those moments, my mind relaxed enough to let go of the worries and the stresses long enough so I could once again take pleasure in the act of reading.

In terms of exercise, it is only now, over seven years on from when Jo was diagnosed, that I'm able to consistently swim, run and cycle again. I do all of those things at a much more leisurely pace than I used to and purely as a way of maintaining overall health. However, the fact that I'm once again able to factor routine exercise into my life has been of significant benefit to me mentally, not just because of the relationship between exercise and mental health but as another personal marker that I can still do those things.

After Jo died, I quickly lost all desire to be downstairs in the house on my own after my daughters had gone to bed. I looked forward to their bedtime because it meant I could turn all the lights off and just sit on my bed. I didn't feel like I was wallowing or shutting myself away, it just felt like something I wanted to do. I found comfort there; I was physically close to my daughters and it was a place where I felt close to Jo. I had no interest in watching TV downstairs or listening to the radio. I dabbled in box set episodes on my iPad but could never settle on one I wanted to commit to. I watched the news with little interest and tried to find documentaries that would hold my attention. This was also the time when I made my futile attempts to read. There is no doubt that part of the reason I did this was because I was physically exhausted and my body was craving the time when I could just sit or lie on the bed and do nothing. My mind didn't even want the distraction that a blockbuster boxset or a mid-week football game would provide. That is understandable, because that was when the reality of losing Jo was really taking route and I was experiencing a plethora of emotions. I had my daughters' welfare, wellbeing and grief to deal with. Having three daughters at different ages and with differing personalities meant that I had to talk to and handle each of them differently as their needs demanded. It's no wonder that all I wanted to do in the evenings was go to my bedroom and simply stop. Because I was so tired, falling to sleep wasn't a problem. However, it did mean I woke up early and usually to a degree that meant falling back to sleep was not an option. We all know the frustration of feeling fully awake at four am and the tricks and mind-games you employ to try and lull yourself back to sleep. At that stage, none of those tricks worked for me.

The issue with this evening routine was that it became a long-term habit. I felt the need to get the housework done and everything ready for the following day before I took my daughters up to start their bedtime. The washing up was done and put away, clothes had been emptied from the tumble dryer and put away, if it was a packed lunch day the following day, they had been made. School bags had been packed and uniforms hung out. I acknowledge that this was partly me being regimented and organised and doing what I needed to do in order to get the girls out of the door on time the following morning. However, my desire to get all of those jobs done in the period after dinner and before seven o'clock, was so that when we went upstairs, I could turn the lights off and wouldn't need to go back downstairs.

I never felt doing that was particularly psychologically damaging and I wasn't consciously shutting myself away; after all, there was no one downstairs I was avoiding being with. But, as that habit lasted over two years, I did realise it was a routine I needed to break. I set a plan to break the cycle in small steps. One day a week I'd leave the housework for later in the evening. Then I'd add in listening to a radio show or committing to a TV programme or boxset episode that I was only allowed to watch downstairs and not on my iPad whilst sitting on my bed. It didn't take long to break the habit and I quickly enjoyed mixing up my own evening routine and, on the nights when I felt particularly tired, I would still relax in my bedroom after my daughters had gone to bed. But, a healthier balance had formed, and, importantly, the enjoyment of having my own space to relax in started to become a feeling I enjoyed having again.

*

Taking all of the above into account, the most significant physical impact I experienced, and the moment which had the most profound impact on me psychologically, occurred during my first week back in the work office after a three-month period of bereavement leave.

I previously mentioned that I knew I wasn't mentally ready to go back to work. However, as the sole earner, I had no choice. On the day in question, I'd actually had a reasonably positive morning in terms of how I was feeling about work and my ability to concentrate on what I was doing. I'd felt engaged during team meetings and had been contributing constructively in them. When my mind wandered, I focused on bringing my attention back to the current moment so I could re-focus on what was being discussed. This compartmentalisation of my life was something I spent a lot of time trying to master.

My home life was focused on me and my daughters readjusting to our new family dynamic and life without Jo. I tried as much as possible to put that to one side when I was at work as I wanted to do my job as effectively as possible.

Lunch that day, as it did almost every day, consisted of a short walk to a sandwich shop under the building and then it was back to the office for another meeting. When that finished, I settled at my desk to write a report. After about half an hour, as I was still typing on the computer keyboard, I suddenly stood up, powered down my computer and grabbed my bag that was under the desk. And then I stopped, aware at what I'd done. I looked at my watch. 2:45pm and a deeply engrained flight or fight response had kicked in. For the majority of the time that Jo was ill, 2:45pm would be the time I called her to see if she needed me to go home to help out when the girls got home from school, or it would be my cut off point for leaving work if I knew beforehand that I needed to get home. On that particular day, even though Jo had been dead for over three months, my sub-conscious reaction was so deeply engrained that I had the same response. My brain told my body that it needed to still do what it had been doing for so long – get home quickly so I could help at home with the girls; even though I had care in place for them so I could work full days in the office.

During the period of my life when I swam competitively, I spent years doing morning training when I needed to get up at 5:30am. After I started regularly waking up at that time, it didn't take long for my body to adjust so I didn't need to rely on my alarm clock. My internal body clock consistently woke me up a few minutes before the alarm went off. This reaction was similar. My sub-conscious self was in control over what

I was doing. One part of my brain had been concentrating on work material and I had been physically typing on a keyboard; however, my body was still full of the tension and responses that manifest in the flight or fight state in which I'd been living for so long. That moment dramatically highlighted to me the impact the trauma of the previous four years had on me. Things had to change—I had to change—because I became acutely aware that my mind had still not fully processed what had happened and certainly hadn't "let go" enough for it to have started to recover.

*

Reflecting on how those physical and psychological symptoms affected me, I realise that until Jo's diagnosis, I was a relatively confident and positive person. I was happy and content with life. I had an amazing family life which I found deeply fulfilling. I enjoyed work, was fit and healthy and I enjoyed being with friends and was fairly confident in my surroundings, be it professionally or socially. That all changed after Jo got ill and all those positive traits flipped upside down – and they did so very quickly. However, it was very important for me to be able to pinpoint and acknowledge the moment when the negative emotions started to take root. Everything had been fine until the day of Jo's diagnosis, so it was clear to me that what I was feeling was driven purely by the emotions that subsequently followed. There was nothing wrong with me, but a different part of my psyche had taken control. It was perfectly normal to not be feeling happy and to feel as if I wasn't coping. That is the impact a trauma can have on someone and how much it can affect a person's entire psyche.

Part Three

The Resilient Self – You Are Much More Resilient Than You Are Aware of

I've already mentioned that when I think back on certain events over the past seven years, it often feels like it was someone else who experienced them. That was certainly the case during the three-month period of bereavement leave I took from work. There was the personal recognition of the reason I was off work, the worries for my family going forward, the impact on the immediate and long-term future of my daughters. I had concerns about how work viewed me whilst I was off and how I was going to be viewed and treated when I returned. I also recognised the dramatic impact Jo's death had on friends and our extended family. Everything and everyone was in my thoughts and being able to navigate myself through that period of time was extremely difficult. There were practical challenges every day. I had to register the death, converse with banks and utility companies to change the name on bills and accounts, do the food shopping and a whole host of other tasks. It's no wonder my body created a defence mechanism where a psychological barrier was formed so I could physically perform those tasks after such a life-changing event. I don't understand the science behind it, but that was the period of time when I physically did things but had little emotional recognition as to what I was doing, and I certainly didn't feel like I was living in the present moment. No wonder that it now feels like it was someone else doing those things, because, in a way, it wasn't me – not the "normal" me anyway.

*

Jo had been clear in her wish that she wanted her funeral to be more of a celebration of life than a traditional service and she knew where she wanted it to take place. The rest of the plans she left to me.

Writing the eulogy, speaking to family, sending out invitations, selecting a venue for the wake, choosing photos, the casket, the flowers, the music to be played during the service, meeting the celebrant. All of these tasks had to be done relatively quickly after Jo died and each of them took a considerable amount of emotional energy, and collectively they were exhausting. The day of the funeral was a hot summer's day and I managed to deliver the eulogy and be as attentive as I could be to the guests. I didn't feel as though I wanted to rush through the day and get it over with but I certainly felt a sense of relief when it was over. Jo deserved it to be, not only a day of memorial, but also one where her life was celebrated. Achieving that for her will always remain a significant personal achievement.

Jo also knew where she wanted to be laid to rest and I chose a plot for her in a protected woodland cemetery. I chose a sapling tree that was planted at her plot and it is somewhere

where my daughters and I can go as a family and the girls can go on their own later in their lives. The intention was for them to grow with the tree and be somewhere that will provide them with a place to reflect and remember their mum.

It was around this time that I vividly remember telling myself that if I could manage to do everything that I did after Jo died, then I could handle anything. In essence, I was trying to tell myself that I was resilient. However, it is one thing telling yourself something but quite another actually believing it or fundamentally understanding what it means.

*

I've already given examples as to how going back to work affected me. My confidence was rock bottom, I was concerned as to how I was viewed, and I felt too removed from home and my daughters. It was a relatively easy transition when I dropped them at school, and they knew I was going to be working from home. It was a very difficult adjustment when I was wearing my suit and they knew I was going to catch a train to London after the school run. Even though they were at school for the day and then being taken care of until I got home, my desire to remain physically close to them was intense and that added to the difficulty of my transition back to work.

I had to find some coping mechanisms to help me get to the station, get on the train and physically do the commute. When I was on the train, memories came flooding back. When I met Jo, I was living in North London, and she was living in an Essex town called Billericay. She moved in with me after about a year and then we started on the young couple journey.

Our first rented flat together and then the first flat we bought. After six years, we decided to make the move back towards Billericay to be closer to Jo's family and to find more affordable housing as the idea of starting a family was growing and we wanted more for our money than we could afford where we'd been living. And so it transpired that the commuter train I now had to take to London after losing her, was the one we took together for three years until our first daughter was born.

That memory was triggered every time I got on the train and that was when I started to listen to audiobooks and look at family photos, trying to find something to distract me and focus on something positive. Before Jo died, I had been able to carry on being effective and confident at work and the daily commute was second nature, even though I had a mind full of worry and concern. I was able to compartmentalise my life inside and outside of work. One morning, close to when Jo's health started to rapidly deteriorate, I conducted two interviews at work, both lasting over an hour and a half. Then I immediately left the office, did the commute home, collected Jo and took her to the hospital to receive a set of scan and treatment results which showed that she only had weeks left to live.

After Jo died, all of the mental coping mechanisms and confidence I had previously displayed, disappeared. My previous self had altered and I was now in a new cycle of worry and concern. The angst over Jo's illness had gone but I was at an early stage of the grieving process and now the concerns were over how I was going to re-build at work, how was I going to be viewed by colleagues, could I even do the commute to the office? I had been at the company for twenty years and I constantly told myself things like, 'It's only work,' 'You can do this,' 'You've done it before so you can do it again.' However, as I've said previously, it's one thing telling yourself something and altogether another thing believing it, especially when your confidence and self-esteem is at rock bottom. Going through a trauma or living with negative emotions damages the confidence and feelings of self-appreciation and self-worth. And sitting on a train or in an office, telling myself repeatedly, 'I can do this. Why can't you concentrate? You used to find this easy,' only added to my frustration. I found it hard to accept that I was struggling to concentrate, read, interpret concepts and data as easily as I previously could, and this only increased my mental angst.

*

A new emotion that manifested in the days that followed Jo's death and has re-surfaced at various times since, was guilt. Whether it was during a routine, fairly mundane aspect of daily life or a significant life event or milestone in our daughters' lives; I have had moments where I've felt guilty. In the immediate aftermath of the funeral, even taking a shower, going for a walk, doing the school run, paying a bill, doing the food shop, eating a meal – everything triggered a guilt response as Jo could never do those things again. I was still here to experience daily life and a future with our daughters, and I felt guilty that Jo wasn't. The experience of that emotion on such a frequent basis and over "normal" daily tasks didn't last too long, but it lasted longer as an emotional response when more significant events took place.

Jo died a few weeks before the start of the school summer holiday and for the whole of that year she promised our eldest daughter that she could get her ears pierced when the school term had finished. I didn't want to break that promise so I booked an appointment for her to have it done on the first day of the holiday. That was the first time I consciously felt a huge wave of guilt that it should have been Jo taking her.

The first day back at school for the next academic year was my youngest daughter's first day in primary school and there were a lot of parents in the playground from my elder two daughters' classes that I hadn't seen since before Jo died, or since her funeral. Doing the school run was familiar to me and had been a frequent part of my daily routine throughout Jo's illness. However, that first day back triggered not only a guilt response that Jo was no longer part of this daily routine, but also a feeling of concern as to how I was going to do this every morning while my daughters were at school. Doing three lots of hair, helping them get ready, making breakfast and then off to school before I went to work. That was going to be how I started the day, with no one to help. I was a single parent. What if I wasn't well? Who could help them get ready or take them to school? I knew I had my parents who I could call on and local friends to rely on if I needed help with a pick-up. But the realisation that I was now on my own made me feel vulnerable and took a considerable amount of time to adjust to.

What helped me the most during this period of adjustment was the knowledge that I had a network of amazing friends who lived locally and also my parents who had made the move from the north-west of the country so they could be closer to me and their granddaughters. Despite it taking a long time to get accustomed to being the only person in the house with my daughters, and all the practicalities and challenges that family life brings; the knowledge of having a support network close by was immensely comforting. For a long time, it was that knowledge that made me able to relax at night and quash any feelings of anxiety that frequently arose when the lights had gone off upstairs. Jo had only been in the hospice for a couple of weeks before she died, and, apart from a short stay in hospital, she'd remained at home throughout her illness. That is something we were both immensely grateful for as she got to spend the vast majority of her time in the comfort of her home with her family. Even though towards the end of her life she was unable to help with our daughters or do any practical tasks around the house, she was still there with us and her presence was of huge comfort to me as I juggled our lives. I constantly felt like I was spinning plates, but she was still there with me in the house and the girls spent a long time simply lying on the bed with her – just being together and enjoying each other's company. And so, it was a huge shock when she suddenly wasn't there anymore.

Everybody's family circumstances and friendship circles are different, but personally, the main factor that helped me though this period was that I had learned to ask for help and, importantly, became comfortable receiving help. I admit that this didn't come easily to me at first. After Jo's diagnosis, I tried to do everything on my own for too long. Friends constantly said to me, 'We are here for you, Jo and the girls. Whatever you need, just ask.' A couple of years into Jo's illness, my parents made the move to be closer to us. But I found it hard to ask for help. Perhaps it was because my natural instinct was to try and prove to Jo, and myself, that I could cope. Perhaps it was also because until Jo's illness got to the stage when organs started to fail and she became bed-ridden, she desperately wanted to carry on doing as much as possible, whether on her own or with me to help. It felt like if I asked for frequent help it would in some way feel like we'd given up and accepted that Jo could no longer do her role as a mother. For those reasons, I don't regret not asking for help earlier, although I do realise that friends and family could see that I needed it.

What I am certain of is that the support me and my daughters have had from our network of friends and family has been the reason why I've been able to adjust to life as a single parent. It was only because I started to ask for help and became comfortable accepting it that made this support network so robust and reliable. It is impossible to overestimate how important that has been for me; knowing that I am not alone and that help is always close by.

I am also certain of something else that is a crucial aspect to everything I have experienced and perhaps the central message of the whole book. For about six years and for all the examples I've given previously, the very last thing I felt was resilient. However, in practise, that is exactly what I had been in virtually every aspect of my life. I did manage to be a husband, carer, dad, worker and housekeeper. My effectiveness at all those things varied significantly over time, however, I can say that I did all of those roles to the best of my ability. I did put a suit on, I did go to the station after the school run and I did do the commute to work. At a time when my confidence was at its lowest point, I did attend work meetings and contribute positively. I was being resilient in all aspects of life and showing the inner strength to just carry on, to keep going through all the self-doubt and concern. I may have felt like a changed person and my mind might have been consumed with negative emotions and distractions – but I had still been resilient.

Part Four

Rebuilding and Growing Stronger

After Jo died, all the professional support and advice I was given on how best to support my daughters centred on one core aspect. To maintain as much normality and stability for them as possible. This was a period of time when the routine of school, interacting with friends and teachers, attending their usual after school and weekend activities, was going to be hugely important for them. As previously mentioned, school summer holidays started two weeks after Jo died and that coincided with my period of bereavement leave from work. It was an important time for us, not only grieving, but also laying the foundation for our new family dynamic. The girls went back to school in September and enjoyed regaining that routine and being able to see their friends on a daily basis. None of them had become reserved in attitude or expression and we all talked openly about how we were feeling – all of which gave me some comfort that they were handling the situation as well as could be expected. I went back to work in the October and, as well as the issues this caused me, my daughters found this separation adjustment difficult. However, the routine, familiarity and support of teachers and friends helped with this.

And then, seven months after Jo died, when my whole focus was on maintaining normality, we entered a national lockdown due to the COVID 19 pandemic and all of that stability and routine disappeared. Most of us could probably write a book on our experiences and the individual challenges we faced during lockdown, and for me, the juggling act of home-schooling three grieving daughters, working full-time, trying to keep a house going and grieving myself during a period of uncertainly was a hugely difficult task. My parents had moved to the area in order to help, however we barely saw each other in person that year due to us adhering to the guidelines of protecting family members. Three things made navigating that year possible for me. After an initial period of time when we were totally alone, I was able to form a support bubble with a nanny who had been providing childcare for me whilst I was at work. She could come and help with practical tasks with the girls whilst I spent part of the day working. The second reason was down to resilience, the ability to keep going when I was exhausted and catching up with work late at night or trying to rationalise the global pandemic focused news broadcasts when I was alone with no one to discuss the issues with. Thirdly, and crucially, I found a positive focus that transformed my mindset amid the significant uncertainty the pandemic created.

In mid-May 2020, a couple of months into lockdown, I reached a low point psychologically. I was missing Jo and had become acutely aware of the gap her death had left in mine and our daughters' lives. It was becoming apparent that the pandemic was more severe than previously forecast, or publicised, and that lockdown was not going to be a short-term event. That made my concerns grow, not only over the impact on my daughters' education but what the effect on them would be of the breakdown of everything that had been expressed as being vital to their well-being. I was becoming mentally fatigued after working late into the night to catch up on work, and with no end of that routine in sight, it was psychologically draining.

And then, one evening when I was serving dinner, my eldest daughter was being very quiet and looking glum. I asked if she was okay and she simply replied, 'I'm okay, I just want to hug Mummy.' I gave her a hug and served dinner but now it was me who fell quiet as my mind raced. Despite all the negative emotions that had been overwhelming me for so long, that phrase triggered something new, certainly an emotion I hadn't experienced for a long time. For a few weeks, I'd been researching books to help my daughters during their grieving process. A lot of them had been written by clinical professionals, and, although I could fully appreciate the importance of the books and the messages they were expressing, I didn't feel they were appropriate at that time for children of my daughters' ages. That comment from my daughter sparked a motivation to write something of my own to help my children; something that I knew would resonate with them. That night I wrote the draft of, "I Want to Hug Mummy", which is a very personal account of the feelings and emotions my daughters were experiencing at the time. The first draft induced a powerful wave of emotions as I was writing purely from experience and observation of my daughters. I knew it was going to be emotionally challenging to finish the book but, crucially, I also now had a purpose, a desire to complete something that provided me with a very positive focus. The energy that purpose gave to me was significant and, shortly after completing the final draft of that book, I wrote another called, "It's Okay to Feel Happy". The idea for the second book stemmed from a holiday me and my daughters went on over the Christmas before lockdown. It had been an important holiday because I proved to myself that I could cope on my own taking the girls on an overseas holiday and it was important that they realised it was okay for us to carry on experiencing new things and doing the things we'd previously done with their mum. It also uncovered some of the thoughts and emotions my daughters were experiencing at the time, and it allowed us to talk about those feelings. It was the first time my daughters had been on a skiing holiday and after the first day, when we were back in the hotel room getting ready for dinner, my eldest daughter became deeply upset and was inconsolable for a considerable period of time. After I sat hugging her and she'd calmed down enough to talk, she explained that she had a horrible feeling in her stomach. She'd had a really fun day and said that skiing was the most fun she'd ever had. But she didn't want to feel like that because Mummy wasn't there to experience it with us. Hearing your seven-year-old daughter explain the feeling of guilt was very upsetting but also extremely important for me to start to comprehend the depth of what my daughters were feeling. It was also a starkly impactful reminder that I was going to have to be mindful at all times as to what each of my daughters was thinking and feeling. Throughout the time that's followed the loss of their mum, I've tried as much as possible to listen and understand things from their point of view. That is at the heart of, "It's Okay to Feel Happy", a book that explores the guilt and anxiety a young child can experience when they lose a parent. I didn't want to write a book telling a child what they should be thinking and feeling; I wanted to write something that explored what they were actually thinking and feeling so they could personally relate to the material.

Although the books were hard to write and edit due to the emotions they raised in me, the act of writing was also cathartic in a number of ways. Seeing my daughters respond positively to them and subsequently receiving feedback that they could help other children and families who had suffered loss, made me feel proud and gave me a little spark of pleasure. I'd promised Jo that at some point I would do something positive from what happened to her. Although I still wished that I was never in the situation where I'd have to write the books, I was pleased that I'd made good on my promise. That was an extremely powerful moment for me because they were feelings and emotions I'd not experienced for a very long time. I was also aware that the only reason I got to feel those self-assuring emotions was because I'd found a positive goal and something that I could always focus on. Even when my personal life was challenging or the outside world was uncertain and destabilising, I now had an underlying positive focus to channel energy towards.

That became a starting point for me. My trigger to, as much as possible, keep focusing on positive actions and to find purpose again. I found it profound how a positive emotion could override—albeit it temporarily at first—emotions of grief, guilt, anxiety and confusion. Profound also because it made me realise that powerfully positive emotions can be experienced even in the most difficult of circumstances. I also recognised that it is our resilient self that can be the most powerful part of us. With the books, I had found a positive focus, however it was the determination and desire to write and edit them until I was happy with them that allowed me to reach the goal of completing them.

My experience during lockdown made me realise that you don't need to be, or feel, fully recovered or back to your old self to be able to enjoy things again, or to start rebuilding yourself and enjoy aspects of life again. No matter what depths you've sunk to emotionally, you can feel better. It is possible to re-build yourself and, no matter what you've gone through, it's okay to feel happy.

We are all different, unique individuals with varying motivations and emotional triggers that personally resonate with us. Finding and unlocking the ones that work for you can be crucial in helping you deal with the periods of time when you are being consumed by negative emotions. For me, having something positive to focus on remains hugely important for my well-being.

*

Post Lockdown

When lockdown started to ease and the world began to open up again, I was able to go out and do more activities with my daughters. This was an important time for us as we'd not had much time to experience life outside of home in the period between Jo dying and lockdown starting. Of all the activities the girls did in the months following "re-opening", a theatre show my youngest two daughters performed in was hugely significant for me because it was another time when I had a moment of self-realisation and awareness.

The show happened nearly two years after Jo died and I thought I was emotionally ready for the performance. Rehearsals had been taking place for many months and I'd seen my daughters numerous times in their costumes. I was full of anticipation whilst sitting in the audience and genuinely excited to see the show. However, the moment the music started and the children paraded onto the stage in full costume, I was instantly overwhelmed with emotion and internally had another brief but powerful moment of "it's not fair, Jo should be here to see this". I felt guilty that it was me sitting in that audience watching our daughters perform. I tried to enjoy the show but struggled to let myself be drawn into it. I'd formed a barrier to keep my emotions suppressed as a packed theatre was not the place for me to burst into tears. Thankfully, that was during the matinee performance. After a short break when I took my daughters to a pizza restaurant, I went back into the theatre much more relaxed, my emotions remained more level and I fully enjoyed the second show. Of course, I would have loved Jo to have seen the performance. However, reminding myself that I couldn't change what had happened or control the past, and that I needed to start taking more pleasure from living in the present moment, made my emotions remain much calmer.

As I sat in bed that night, I reflected on the intensity of the emotions I'd felt during the matinee. Emotions so powerful that I genuinely didn't know if I could stay in the theatre or if I'd have to leave. And contrasting that to how I felt only a couple of hours later, calmly sitting in a relaxed state and thoroughly enjoying the moment.

I realised that, although I hadn't been consciously thinking that I didn't deserve to be happy because of what happened to Jo; it was more that I'd forgotten what it felt like to feel truly happy. That genuine, deep centred feeling of happiness and contentment was something I hadn't felt for a long time. Even when I was socialising with friends, playing with my daughters or watching a film, other emotions had been the dominant factor. However, during those few hours in the theatre, I had fully enjoyed the moment and I had smiled and laughed and not thought about anything else other than what was happening on the stage. And it felt good.

Part Five

Looking Forward

The events that I've documented and reflected on in this book took place over a seven-and-a-half-year period, from the day of Jo's diagnosis to the time of writing. All the events directly influenced the personal and psychological arc that I experienced and shaped the person I have become. The events will influence how I raise my daughters – they have suffered a significant trauma early in their lives and they need to be cared for and nurtured accordingly as they are still children and deserve, like any child, to lead as happy a childhood as possible. Like me, they will be shaped by what has happened to our family. The loss of their mum is irreversible and will clearly have an impact on our psyches as we go through our lives. However, I will not be defined by what has happened and I will do my utmost as a parent to make sure that my daughters do not grow up defined by the loss of their mum. They need to understand what has happened, grow to accept what has happened and be given the chance, just like me, to express their emotions whenever they feel the need. No one should ever feel they have to suppress the emotion they are experiencing; whether the pressure to do so is by social or professional convention. When I suppressed what I was feeling, that was when I did feel defined by what had happened because I had no method of release, and that meant I couldn't live in the present moment. Instead, I was constantly worried about what had happened or what was going to happen. To process the trauma I experienced, I had to live through a cocktail of emotions and then personally develop to a stage where I could recognise the emotions in order to accept them so I could continue to rebuild myself. Emotional symptoms that result from a personal trauma of any sort, or periods in someone's life that are dominated by negative emotions, should not be made into something taboo. If the need is there, anyone should be able to talk openly without feeling that there is a stigma attached to it. Once I realised how important talking is to mental well-being, I started to become more confident in expressing my thoughts and emotions.

When Jo became bed-ridden at home and subsequently moved into the hospice, our friends created a daily rota between them of collecting our daughters in the morning and then dropping them home after school so that I could remain at the hospice. I've mentioned that my parents moved from one side of the country to the other in order to help me and be a closer support to their granddaughters. All of this practical support was, and still is, invaluable. However, what has helped me even more than that, is that they allowed me to talk. I learnt to "open up" and my close friends became even closer and I felt comfortable, at ease and able to talk to them about what was on my mind. That helped me more than I'll ever totally comprehend.

Resilience is at the heart of this book. As individuals, we are all different and have different mental triggers that stimulate us. What surprised me as much as anything I experienced, was how powerful that resilient trait can be and how it can manifest itself when we are at our very lowest point. That certainly happened with me. And it was there, helping me carry on with life, even when I had no acknowledgment of it.

I think my inner resilience was partly formed in childhood. The discipline and routine that years of waking up early to travel to a swimming pool and diving into cold water for a two-hour training session, would certainly have built up a core physical and mental resilience. Over the last seven years, I'm sure that helped me as my mind had previous experience of pushing though and carrying on when things got hard. I recognise that I am equating something that was physically demanding with the period in my life that was the most emotionally challenging. None-the-less, I believe that the resilient trait I built up during childhood, helped me as an adult.

My experience also taught me that I didn't have to be doing something physically demanding in order to be resilient. When I found the positive focus of writing the books, I was physically exhausted and unable to exercise. However, it showed emotional resilience to be able to complete the books. Having a goal increased my discipline, which allowed me to write and edit the books when I'd finished work late at night. The consistent focus on something positive gave me more direct appreciation that I was being resilient, and that stemmed from finding one positive thing to focus on. Even if it's hidden or has been suppressed due to a trauma or period when we are experiencing negative emotions; we all have personal motivators, the things that make us tick. Focusing on them can be transformational; once I'd felt the positive emotion that came from it, I wanted to feel that emotion again, which then further increased motivation. It was a positive cycle that I could maintain.

Like everything in life, you have to be proactive and work hard at something you want. I had to work hard at reminding myself that emotions are just that; feelings that come and go which can have profound effects on me physically as well as mentally. Accepting this was difficult because experiencing negative emotions can feel totally overwhelming. But the more I told myself that what I was feeling was totally normal—very unpleasant, but normal—the more I was able to handle the emotion when it occurred. Now, if a period of negative emotion hits, I try and respond by finding something mentally or physically positive to do. A few minutes of calm breathing, using gratitude to remind myself of how many things I have to be truly grateful for. Going for a jog, a swim, a cycle, some gardening, reading, writing, going to Jo's tree and having a chat about how I'm feeling. These all help me.

My emotions still fluctuate, and I certainly have difficult days. However, I also realise that feeling down, anxious, nervous, stressed or guilty is as normal as feeling happy, excited, confident and motivated. It's just a different part of my psyche that has temporarily come to the fore. Rather than avoid it or hide from it, I try to acknowledge the emotions for what they are—a totally normal part of me that ebbs and flows—and then I'm able to move on and continue to rebuild.

I also think that part of my ability to carry on in adversity is a reflection of how Jo lived her life during her illness. She lived for almost four years with incurable cancer, but I never once saw her allow self-pity to overwhelm her. During the eulogy at her funeral, I talked about how Jo chose to live her life, conduct herself and continue to be herself after her diagnosis. That left me in awe every day. I'd never seen anyone exhibit the trait of resilience more than she did, and if it's true that a person strives to manifest personal traits in others that they admire and want to exhibit themselves, then I believe I inherently developed an increased resilience from the way she conducted herself.

I also hope Jo would be proud of me writing this book. It has not been an easy task due to the emotions it has raised in me and the very personal nature of the issues I've talked about. However, as I stated near the start, if my open and honest account can help just one other person who has suffered a trauma of any sort or is living through a period of negative emotions, then it has been well worth the effort and the emotional journey it has taken me on.

THE END

Printed in Great Britain
by Amazon